WRITTEN AND ILLUSTRATED BY MEREDITH POCZKALSKI

COPYRIGHT © 2024 MEREDITH POCZKALSKI. ALL RIGHTS RESERVED. NO PART OF THIS PUBLICATION MAY BE REPRODUCED, DISTRIBUTED, OR TRANSMITTED IN ANY FORM OR BY ANY MEANS, INCLUDING PHOTOCOPYING, RECORDING, OR OTHER ELECTRONIC OR MECHANICAL METHODS, WITHOUT THE PRIOR WRITTEN PERMISSION OF THE AUTHOR.

FIRST U.S. EDITION, 2024

WRITTEN BY MEREDITH POCZKALSKI

30 Day

ACTIONABLE INSIGHTS FROM PERSONAL EXPERIENCE

CHECKLIST

A GUIDE TO BUILDING RESILIENCE AT WORK

NAVIGATE CHALLENGING BEHAVIORS

Use this daily checklist to learn and build on strategies to manage stressful or narcissistic co-workers over a 30-day timeframe. Each day introduces a new concept or activity to progressively help you develop these skills and learn to accept behaviors without damaging effects on your well-being.

EMBRACE THE JOURNEY, TRUST YOUR ABILITIES

Not personalizing difficult behavior is essential. However, it's also crucial to acknowledge your feelings. Remember, it's normal to feel frustrated or upset in such situations. Focusing on the task and not taking their actions personally can help you navigate these feelings.

This book allows you to either choose the activity that best fits your current situation or follow the days sequentially. This flexible approach helps you prioritize your immediate needs, gain a better understanding of your co-workers, manage stress, and protect your emotional well-being. Ultimately, it empowers you to create a more positive, productive workplace while prioritizing your mental health.

REFLECT AND LEARN ✱ **TRUST THE PROCESS** ✱ **FEEL EMPOWERED**

Author's Note | MP

There are many valuable books and guides on navigating career challenges, but what may set this book apart is my firsthand experience. For years, I struggled daily with working alongside a difficult co-worker, constantly reflecting on how to learn and grow from each encounter. Despite reaching out for support, my boss ignored my concerns, and Human Resources seemed more focused on protecting the company than addressing my requests for improvement.

This experience took an emotional toll, prompting me to seek guidance from a career coach and therapist. Their support helped me rebuild my self-esteem and find the courage to set boundaries. It was a long and challenging journey, but I'm grateful I endured it, reflected upon it, and now have the opportunity to share these insights with you. Remember, you are not alone in facing workplace challenges. Each hurdle is an opportunity for growth and resilience. Keep moving forward with determination and self-awareness, and you will emerge more confident on the other side.

This 30-day checklist is designed to equip you with the knowledge, skills, and emotional resilience needed to overcome the challenges posed by a demanding co-worker. Each day's activity or reflection is a step toward a deeper understanding of workplace dynamics, empowering you to foster a more positive and productive work environment.

The checklist is structured to provide flexibility and focus:
- Choose Your Focus: Select the day's activity that aligns with your current needs or challenges.
- Flexibility: There's no need to follow the checklist sequentially—choose the most relevant activity for the day.
- Reflection: After completing each activity, take time to reflect on how it applies to your work environment.
- Apply Learnings: Use the insights gained to better understand co-workers, manage stress, and improve interactions.
- Consistency: Commit to daily engagement to gradually improve workplace dynamics and personal well-being.

With this guide, you'll gain the tools to transform challenges into opportunities, creating a healthier, more fulfilling work experience.

Table of Contents	*1-30* *Recap*

Day 1: Recognizing a difficult co-worker in the workplace
Day 2: Practice deep breathing exercises
Day 3: Identify one boundary you want to set at work
Day 4: Practice using direct language in a conversation
Day 5: Document your interactions with a difficult co-worker
Day 6: Their behavior is about them, not you
Day 7: Talk to a trusted colleague or mentor
Day 8: Prioritize self-care
Day 9: Understanding their perspective
Day 10: Think of two constructive ideas to improve a challenging situation
Day 11: Practice using "I feel" statements in your conversations
Day 12: Commit to keeping your interactions work-related
Day 13: Adjust your expectations about the difficult co-worker's behavior
Day 14: Identify one new stress-relief activity
Day 15: Remind yourself that change is gradual and requires patience
Day 16: Gain constructive feedback from a colleague
Day 17: Engage in a resilience-building activity
Day 18: Lighten the mood with appropriate, cheerful humor
Day 19: Focus on the big picture and let minor irritations go
Day 20: Practice standing your ground firmly yet respectfully
Day 21: Focus on the issue at hand rather than getting drawn into a conflict over control
Day 22: Focus on your professional goals and align your actions with them
Day 23: Plan for potential challenges in an upcoming interaction
Day 24: Minimize unnecessary contact with the problematic co-worker today
Day 25: Review your workplace policies on behavior and conflict resolution
Day 26: Suggest a team project or collective goal to foster teamwork
Day 27: Learn one new conflict resolution technique
Day 28: Write down three things you are grateful for today
Day 29: Adapt your approach based on what works best in a given situation
Day 30: Reflect on your limits and consider if walking away might be necessary

| Day | 1 |

WORK ENVIRONMENT

DAY 1: RECOGNIZING A DIFFICULT CO-WORKER IN THE WORKPLACE

GRANDIOSITY	LACK OF EMPATHY	NEED FOR ADMIRATION
AN INFLATED SENSE OF SELF-IMPORTANCE, WHERE A PERSON EXAGGERATES THEIR ACHIEVEMENTS AND EXPECTS TO BE RECOGNIZED AS SUPERIOR WITHOUT HAVING EARNED IT.	AN INABILITY OR UNWILLINGNESS TO UNDERSTAND OR RELATE TO OTHERS' FEELINGS OR NEEDS.	A CONSTANT DESIRE FOR EXCESSIVE PRAISE AND VALIDATION, OFTEN BECOMING UPSET WHEN THEY'RE NOT THE CENTER OF ATTENTION.

THROUGHOUT THE DAY, OBSERVE YOUR CO-WORKER AND NOTE ANY BEHAVIORS THAT ALIGN WITH THESE TRAITS. PAY ATTENTION TO:
- CONVERSATIONS WHERE SOMEONE OFTEN TALKS ABOUT THEIR OWN ACHIEVEMENTS OR BELITTLES OTHERS.
- SITUATIONS WHERE A CO-WORKER SHOWS LITTLE REGARD FOR OTHERS' FEELINGS OR NEEDS.
- INSTANCES WHERE A PERSON SEEKS CONSTANT PRAISE OR BECOMES UPSET WHEN NOT RECEIVING ATTENTION.

REFLECTION:
- HOW DO THESE BEHAVIORS IMPACT YOUR INTERACTIONS AND WORK ENVIRONMENT?
- IN WHAT WAYS CAN RECOGNIZING THESE TRAITS HELP YOU NAVIGATE DIFFICULT CO-WORKER DYNAMICS MORE EFFECTIVELY?

BY IDENTIFYING THESE BEHAVIORS EARLY ON, YOU'LL BE BETTER EQUIPPED TO MANAGE AND RESPOND TO DIFFICULT INTERACTIONS.

Day 2

STAY CALM

DAY 2: PRACTICE DEEP BREATHING EXERCISES AND MINDFULNESS

OBJECTIVE	ACTIVITY	DEEP BREATHING EXERCISE
LEARN TO MANAGE YOUR STRESS AND STAY CALM WHEN DEALING WITH A DIFFICULT CO-WORKER.	DEEP BREATHING EXERCISES ARE A SIMPLE YET POWERFUL TOOL TO REDUCE STRESS, LOWER ANXIETY, AND PROMOTE A SENSE OF CALM. THESE EXERCISES HELP ACTIVATE THE BODY'S RELAXATION RESPONSE, WHICH COUNTERACTS THE STRESS RESPONSE.	1. FIND A QUIET SPACE 2. SIT COMFORTABLY 3. CLOSE YOUR EYES 4. INHALE DEEPLY THROUGH YOUR NOSE 5. HOLD YOUR BREATH FOR A COUNT OF FOUR 6. EXHALE SLOWLY THROUGH YOUR MOUTH FOR A COUNT OF SIX 7. PAUSE BRIEFLY BEFORE THE NEXT BREATH 8. REPEAT FOR 10 MINUTES, FOCUSING ON THE RHYTHM OF YOUR BREATH

WHENEVER YOU FEEL STRESSED AT WORK, PRACTICE DEEP BREATHING TO REGAIN COMPOSURE. COMBINE THIS WITH OTHER RELAXATION TECHNIQUES LIKE MINDFULNESS OR VISUALIZATION FOR ADDED BENEFITS.

AN EXAMPLE OF MINDFULNESS IS THE "5-4-3-2-1" GROUNDING EXERCISE. FIND A COMFORTABLE PLACE TO SIT AND TAKE A DEEP BREATH:
- OBSERVE FIVE THINGS YOU CAN SEE AROUND YOU. DESCRIBE THEM IN DETAIL.
- IDENTIFY FOUR THINGS YOU CAN TOUCH AND FEEL THEIR TEXTURE.
- NOTICE THREE THINGS YOU CAN HEAR AND FOCUS ON THEIR SOUND.
- ACKNOWLEDGE TWO THINGS YOU CAN SMELL AND BREATHE THEM IN.
- FOCUS ON ONE THING YOU CAN TASTE, OR THINK OF A FAVORITE TASTE.

THIS EXERCISE HELPS GROUND YOU IN THE PRESENT MOMENT AND CAN BE A POWERFUL TOOL TO REDUCE STRESS AND INCREASE AWARENESS.

Day 3

SET BOUNDARIES

DAY 3: IDENTIFY ONE BOUNDARY YOU WANT TO SET AT WORK

OBJECTIVE	ACTIVITY	IDENTIFY AND PLAN COMMUNICATION
ESTABLISH A CLEAR BOUNDARY TO PROTECT YOUR WELL-BEING AND IMPROVE INTERACTIONS WITH A DIFFICULT CO-WORKER.	IDENTIFY ONE SPECIFIC AREA WHERE YOU NEED TO SET A BOUNDARY. THIS COULD BE RELATED TO COMMUNICATION, WORKLOAD, PERSONAL SPACE, OR RESPECT.	CLEARLY DEFINE THE BOUNDARY YOU WANT TO SET. FOR EXAMPLE: • "I WILL NOT ANSWER WORK EMAILS AFTER 6 PM." THINK ABOUT HOW YOU WILL COMMUNICATE THIS BOUNDARY TO YOUR CO-WORKERS. USE ASSERTIVE BUT RESPECTFUL LANGUAGE. FOR EXAMPLE: • "I APPRECIATE YOUR UNDERSTANDING THAT I NEED TO DISCONNECT FROM WORK AFTER 6 PM TO RECHARGE."

CONSIDER HOW SETTING THIS BOUNDARY MIGHT CHANGE YOUR WORK ENVIRONMENT AND INTERACTIONS. REFLECT ON ANY POTENTIAL CHALLENGES YOU MIGHT FACE AND HOW YOU WILL ADDRESS THEM.

CONSISTENTLY ENFORCE YOUR BOUNDARY TO ESTABLISH ITS IMPORTANCE. ENSURE YOUR CO-WORKERS UNDERSTAND YOUR BOUNDARY AND THE REASONS BEHIND IT. BE OPEN TO ADJUSTING YOUR BOUNDARY IF IT'S NOT WORKING AS INTENDED, WHILE STILL MAINTAINING YOUR CORE NEEDS. COMMIT TO TAKING TIME FOR YOURSELF TO STEP AWAY FROM WORK DURING THOSE ESTABLISHED TIMES.

BY SETTING AND MAINTAINING CLEAR BOUNDARIES, YOU CREATE A HEALTHIER WORK ENVIRONMENT WHERE YOU CAN THRIVE EVEN WHEN DEALING WITH A DIFFICULT CO-WORKER.

| Day | 4 |

COMMUNICATE CLEARLY

DAY 4: PRACTICE USING DIRECT LANGUAGE IN A CONVERSATION

OBJECTIVE	ACTIVITY	COMMUNICATE CLEARLY
ENHANCE YOUR ABILITY TO USE CLEAR AND DIRECT LANGUAGE IN CONVERSATIONS.	IDENTIFY AN UPCOMING CONVERSATION OR INTERACTION WHERE YOU CAN PRACTICE USING DIRECT LANGUAGE. THIS COULD BE A MEETING, A CASUAL DISCUSSION, OR AN EMAIL EXCHANGE.	USE "I" STATEMENTS TO EXPRESS YOUR THOUGHTS AND FEELINGS. REFER TO DAY 11 FOR MORE. BE SPECIFIC ABOUT YOUR NEEDS AND EXPECTATIONS. AVOID VAGUE OR PASSIVE LANGUAGE.

DIRECT LANGUAGE IS CONCISE AND TO THE POINT. IT AVOIDS AMBIGUITY AND ENSURES THAT THE MESSAGE IS CLEAR.

PREPARE YOUR MESSAGE:
- IDENTIFY YOUR GOAL: WHAT DO YOU WANT TO ACHIEVE FROM THIS CONVERSATION? BE CLEAR ABOUT YOUR OBJECTIVE.
- PLAN WHAT TO SAY USING DIRECT LANGUAGE. FOR EXAMPLE:
- INSTEAD OF SAYING, "COULD YOU MAYBE FINISH YOUR PART OF THE REPORT SOON?" SAY, "PLEASE COMPLETE YOUR PART OF THE REPORT BY FRIDAY AT 2 PM CST SO WE CAN STAY ON SCHEDULE."

IF POSSIBLE, PRACTICE YOUR MESSAGE WITH A TRUSTED FRIEND OR COLLEAGUE. GET FEEDBACK ON YOUR CLARITY AND ADJUST AS NEEDED. USE YOUR PREPARED MESSAGE IN THE IDENTIFIED CONVERSATION. PAY ATTENTION TO HOW YOUR CO-WORKER RESPONDS AND HOW THE INTERACTION UNFOLDS.

Day	5

DOCUMENT EVERYTHING

DAY 5: DOCUMENT YOUR INTERACTIONS WITH A DIFFICULT CO-WORKER

OBJECTIVE	ACTIVITY	DOCUMENT
MAINTAIN CLEAR AND FACTUAL RECORDS OF YOUR INTERACTIONS TO PROTECT YOURSELF AND PROVIDE EVIDENCE IF NEEDED.	SET TIME ASIDE TO KEEP A CLEAR AND OBJECTIVE RECORD OF YOUR INTERACTIONS.	1. RECORD THE DATE, TIME, AND FACTS OF EACH INTERACTION. 2. NOTE ANY WITNESSES PRESENT. 3. SEND YOURSELF AN EMAIL OR TEXT WITH THE DOCUMENTED DETAILS. 4. STAY OBJECTIVE: KEEP YOUR EMOTIONS OUT OF THE DOCUMENTATION AND FOCUS ON FACTUAL INFORMATION.

REVIEW YOUR DOCUMENTATION REGULARLY TO IDENTIFY ANY PATTERNS OR RECURRING ISSUES. CONSIDER HOW DETAILED RECORDS MIGHT ASSIST IN ADDRESSING PROBLEMS WITH A CO-WORKER OR DISCUSSIONS WITH MANAGEMENT.

AUTHOR'S NOTE: I WORKED WITH A CO-WORKER WHO FREQUENTLY CALLED TO SHARE GOSSIP SHE HAD HEARD FROM THE TEAM. ONE AFTERNOON, SHE SAID, "I HEAR THAT YOU DON'T SPEAK VERY HIGHLY OF ME TO THESE PEOPLE." I CORRECTED HER, CLARIFYING THAT I HAD NEVER SPOKEN ABOUT HER TO ANYONE. ONCE I REALIZED THIS WAS A RECURRING CYCLE, HAPPENING ALMOST DAILY, I STARTED EMAILING HER RECAPS OF OUR PHONE CONVERSATIONS WITH OUR BOSS COPIED IN. THE PHONE CALLS STOPPED IMMEDIATELY, AND WE WERE ABLE TO FOCUS ON NEW AND STRONGER GOALS RATHER THAN DISAGREEING DUE TO FALSE INFORMATION.

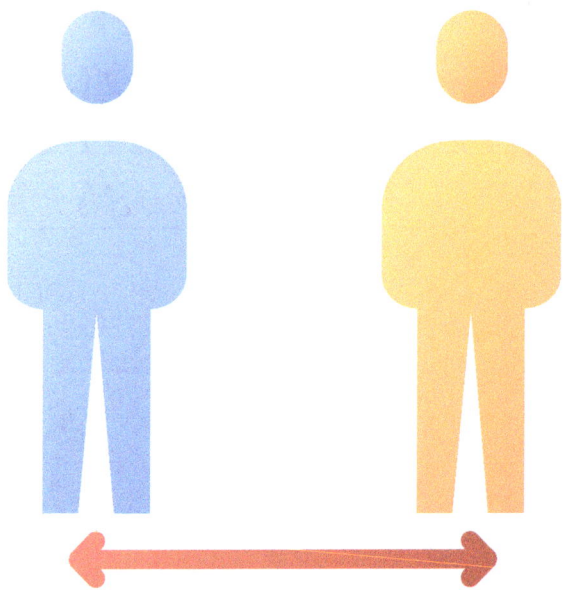

Day	6

AVOID PERSONALIZATION

DAY 6: THEIR BEHAVIOR IS ABOUT THEM, NOT YOU

OBJECTIVE	ACTIVITY	REFLECT, REFRAME
UNDERSTAND THAT NEGATIVE BEHAVIOR FROM A CO-WORKER IS A REFLECTION OF THEIR ISSUES, NOT A JUDGMENT OF YOU.	AVOID PERSONALIZATION TO HELP MAINTAIN YOUR SELF-ESTEEM AND EMOTIONAL WELL-BEING. RESPOND CALMLY AND EFFECTIVELY.	REFLECT ON RECENT INTERACTIONS: • CONSIDER HOW THEIR BEHAVIOR MIGHT BE INFLUENCED BY THEIR OWN ISSUES, INSECURITIES, OR EXTERNAL FACTORS. REFRAME YOUR THOUGHTS: • REMIND YOURSELF THAT THEIR BEHAVIOR IS ABOUT THEM, NOT YOU. • FOCUS ON YOUR STRENGTHS AND MAINTAIN YOUR SELF-WORTH.

AVOID SHARING YOUR PERSONAL INFORMATION WITH A DIFFICULT CO-WORKER. FOCUS CONVERSATIONS STRICTLY ON WORK-RELATED MATTERS.

REFLECT:
- IDENTIFY ANY RECURRING ISSUES WITH OTHERS AS WELL, NOT JUST WITH YOU.
- DOCUMENT WHY THEIR BEHAVIOR IS A REFLECTION OF THEIR PERSONAL ISSUES.
- CONSIDER HOW THIS UNDERSTANDING HELPS YOU DEPERSONALIZE THEIR ACTIONS AND REDUCE THE EMOTIONAL IMPACT ON YOU.

AUTHOR'S NOTE: WORKING WITH A CO-WORKER WHO USED INTIMIDATION TO MASK LOW SELF-ESTEEM WAS CHALLENGING, BUT IT TAUGHT ME THE IMPORTANCE OF SETTING BOUNDARIES. BY DOCUMENTING OUR INTERACTIONS AND REMAINING CALM, I PROTECTED MYSELF FROM THEIR NEGATIVITY AND MAINTAINED MY PROFESSIONALISM. THIS APPROACH ALLOWED ME TO NAVIGATE OUR INTERACTIONS EFFECTIVELY AND FOCUS MY ENERGY ON MORE POSITIVE AND PRODUCTIVE ASPECTS OF MY WORK.

Day	7

SEEK SUPPORT

DAY 7: TALK TO A TRUSTED COLLEAGUE OR MENTOR

OBJECTIVE	ACTIVITY	CHOOSE, SEEK, LISTEN, CONSIDER
GAIN PERSPECTIVE AND ADVICE BY DISCUSSING YOUR SITUATION WITH SOMEONE YOU TRUST.	EXPLAIN THE CHALLENGES YOU'RE FACING. BE HONEST ABOUT YOUR FEELINGS AND SPECIFIC INCIDENTS THAT HAVE OCCURRED.	• CHOOSE SOMEONE WHO IS UNDERSTANDING, SUPPORTIVE, AND CAN OFFER VALUABLE INSIGHTS. • SEEK ADVICE ON HOW TO HANDLE THE SITUATION EFFECTIVELY. • LISTEN TO FEEDBACK. • CONSIDER HOW THEIR PERSPECTIVE CAN HELP YOU APPROACH THE SITUATION DIFFERENTLY.

DOCUMENT KEY TAKEAWAYS FROM THE CONVERSATION. THINK ABOUT HOW THE SUPPORT AND ADVICE CAN BE APPLIED TO IMPROVE YOUR INTERACTIONS AND WELL-BEING.

REFLECT:
• HOW DID DISCUSSING YOUR SITUATION WITH SOMEONE YOU TRUST MAKE YOU FEEL?
• WHAT NEW INSIGHTS OR STRATEGIES DID YOU GAIN FROM THIS CONVERSATION?

AUTHOR'S NOTE: WHEN SEEKING SUPPORT, AVOID GOSSIPING OR VENTING EMOTIONALLY. STICK TO SHARING FACTS ABOUT YOUR INTERACTIONS WITH THE DIFFICULT CO-WORKER. THIS APPROACH ENSURES THAT THE CONVERSATION REMAINS PROFESSIONAL AND PRODUCTIVE. BY FOCUSING ON THE FACTS, YOU ALLOW YOUR COLLEAGUE OR MENTOR TO OFFER CLEAR-HEADED ADVICE AND SUPPORT, WHICH CAN HELP YOU DEVELOP EFFECTIVE STRATEGIES FOR SITUATION MANAGING.

Day 8

BUILD EMOTIONAL RESILIENCE - EXERCISE

DAY 8: PRIORITIZE SELF-CARE

OBJECTIVE	ACTIVITY	COMMIT
STRENGTHEN YOUR EMOTIONAL RESILIENCE BY INCORPORATING SELF-CARE INTO YOUR ROUTINE.	SET ASIDE 30 MINUTES FOR AN EXERCISE SESSION. CHOOSE AN ACTIVITY YOU ENJOY, SUCH AS WALKING, JOGGING, YOGA, OR A FITNESS CLASS.	TREAT THIS TIME AS AN IMPORTANT APPOINTMENT AND STICK TO IT.

REFLECT:
- HOW DID THE EXERCISE SESSION MAKE YOU FEEL PHYSICALLY AND EMOTIONALLY?
- DID IT HELP ALLEVIATE ANY STRESS OR TENSION FROM DEALING WITH A DIFFICULT CO-WORKER?
- WHAT ADJUSTMENTS CAN YOU MAKE TO ENSURE REGULAR SELF-CARE PRACTICES LIKE EXERCISE?

BY PRIORITIZING SELF-CARE, YOU ENHANCE YOUR EMOTIONAL RESILIENCE, ENABLING YOU TO MANAGE WORKPLACE CHALLENGES MORE EFFECTIVELY AND MAINTAIN OVERALL WELL-BEING.

| Day | 9 |

PRACTICE EMPATHY

DAY 9: UNDERSTANDING THEIR PERSPECTIVE

OBJECTIVE	ACTIVITY	CONSIDER
DEVELOP EMPATHY BY UNDERSTANDING THEIR PERSPECTIVE IN A SPECIFIC INTERACTION.	RECALL A RECENT INTERACTION WITH A DIFFICULT CO-WORKER THAT WAS CHALLENGING OR FRUSTRATING.	PUT YOURSELF IN THEIR SHOES AND CONSIDER WHY THEY MAY HAVE REACTED OR BEHAVED IN THAT WAY. THINK ABOUT THEIR MOTIVATIONS, FEELINGS, AND POSSIBLE EXTERNAL FACTORS INFLUENCING THEIR BEHAVIOR. DOCUMENT YOUR THOUGHTS ON THEIR PERSPECTIVE AND WHAT YOU'VE LEARNED FROM THIS EXERCISE.

REFLECT:
- HOW DID PRACTICING EMPATHY CHANGE YOUR UNDERSTANDING OF THE INTERACTION?
- DID IT PROVIDE ANY INSIGHTS INTO THEIR BEHAVIOR OR MOTIVATIONS?
- HOW CAN UNDERSTANDING THEIR PERSPECTIVE HELP IMPROVE FUTURE INTERACTIONS?

PRACTICING EMPATHY FOSTERS UNDERSTANDING AND CAN LEAD TO MORE CONSTRUCTIVE INTERACTIONS.

AUTHOR'S NOTE: THIS ACTIVITY HAS BEEN ONE OF THE MOST CHALLENGING FOR ME, AS I OFTEN STRUGGLE TO UNDERSTAND CERTAIN PERSONALITY TRAITS. HOWEVER, MAKING AN EFFORT TO UNDERSTAND CAN IMPROVE HOW YOU THINK AND RESPOND TO NEGATIVITY. STAY CALM DURING THIS ACTIVITY AND FOCUS ON KEEPING YOUR THOUGHTS POSITIVE. FOR EXAMPLE, AFTER REFLECTING ON A PAST CONVERSATION, I REALIZED THE PERSON HAD LOW SELF-ESTEEM AND FELT THE NEED TO BELITTLE OTHERS TO BOOST THEIR OWN SENSE OF IMPORTANCE.

Day	10

FOCUS ON SOLUTIONS
DAY 10: THINK OF TWO CONSTRUCTIVE IDEAS TO IMPROVE A CHALLENGING SITUATION

OBJECTIVE	ACTIVITY	GENERATE SOLUTIONS
SHIFT YOUR FOCUS FROM PROBLEMS TO SOLUTIONS BY GENERATING CONSTRUCTIVE IDEAS FOR IMPROVING CHALLENGING SITUATIONS.	CHOOSE A RECENT INTERACTION OR ONGOING ISSUE AT WORK.	THINK OF TWO CONSTRUCTIVE IDEAS TO IMPROVE THE SITUATION. FOR EXAMPLE, SUGGEST A REGULAR TEAM MEETING TO ADDRESS COMMUNICATION ISSUES AND STAY POSITIVE. YOU COULD ALSO PROPOSE A NEW WORKFLOW TO STREAMLINE TASKS AND REDUCE CONFLICT OR OVERLAPS.

IMPLEMENT AND OBSERVE:
PUT YOUR IDEAS INTO ACTION AND OBSERVE THEIR IMPACT. STAY CONSISTENT.

REFLECT:
- HOW DID FOCUSING ON SOLUTIONS CHANGE YOUR PERSPECTIVE ON THE SITUATION?
- DID THE SOLUTIONS YOU IMPLEMENTED IMPROVE THE SITUATION? IF SO, HOW?
- WHAT DID YOU LEARN ABOUT PROBLEM-SOLVING AND CONSTRUCTIVE THINKING THROUGH THIS PROCESS?

BY FOCUSING ON SOLUTIONS, YOU CAN ACTIVELY IMPROVE CHALLENGING SITUATIONS AND FOSTER A MORE POSITIVE AND PRODUCTIVE WORK ENVIRONMENT.

Day 11

USE "I" STATEMENTS

DAY 11: PRACTICE USING "I FEEL" STATEMENTS IN YOUR CONVERSATIONS

OBJECTIVE	ACTIVITY	IDENTIFY AND FRAME
IMPROVE COMMUNICATION AND REDUCE DEFENSIVENESS BY USING "I" STATEMENTS IN YOUR CONVERSATIONS.	"I" STATEMENTS EXPRESS YOUR FEELINGS AND THOUGHTS WITHOUT BLAMING OR CRITICIZING OTHERS. THEY HELP YOU COMMUNICATE MORE EFFECTIVELY AND REDUCE DEFENSIVENESS.	CHOOSE A RECENT OR UPCOMING CONVERSATION WHERE YOU CAN PRACTICE USING "I" STATEMENTS. FRAME YOUR THOUGHTS AND FEELINGS USING "I" STATEMENTS. ○ INSTEAD OF SAYING, "YOU NEVER LISTEN TO ME," SAY, "I FEEL UNHEARD WHEN MY IDEAS ARE OVERLOOKED."

PRACTICE:
USE THE ABOVE STATEMENT AS AN EXAMPLE IN YOUR IDENTIFIED CONVERSATION AND OBSERVE THE RESPONSE.

REFLECT:
- HOW DID USING "I" STATEMENTS AFFECT THE CONVERSATION?
- DID IT HELP IN REDUCING DEFENSIVENESS AND FOSTERING UNDERSTANDING?
- WHAT DID YOU LEARN ABOUT YOUR COMMUNICATION STYLE AND ITS IMPACT ON OTHERS?

BY PRACTICING "I" STATEMENTS, YOU CAN COMMUNICATE MORE OPENLY AND CONSTRUCTIVELY, LEADING TO MORE POSITIVE INTERACTIONS AND RELATIONSHIPS.

Day | 12

STAY PROFESSIONAL

DAY 12: COMMIT TO KEEPING YOUR INTERACTIONS WORK-RELATED

OBJECTIVE	ACTIVITY	PREPARE
MAINTAIN PROFESSIONALISM BY FOCUSING ON WORK-RELATED TOPICS DURING INTERACTIONS.	MAKE A CONSCIOUS DECISION TO KEEP YOUR INTERACTIONS STRICTLY WORK-RELATED.	PLAN AHEAD FOR CONVERSATIONS OR MEETINGS. OUTLINE THE WORK-RELATED TOPICS YOU NEED TO DISCUSS. AVOID PERSONAL COMMENTS OR GETTING DRAWN INTO NON-WORK-RELATED DISCUSSIONS.

STAY FOCUSED:
- DURING INTERACTIONS, STEER THE CONVERSATION BACK TO WORK IF IT STARTS TO VEER OFF-TOPIC
- USE PHRASES LIKE, "LET'S GET BACK TO DISCUSSING THE PROJECT" OR "THANK YOU FOR THAT INFORMATION. HOW DOES THIS RELATE TO OUR CURRENT TASK?"

REFLECT:
- HOW DID STAYING PROFESSIONAL AFFECT YOUR INTERACTIONS?
- DID IT HELP IN REDUCING CONFLICTS OR MISUNDERSTANDINGS?
- WHAT DID YOU LEARN ABOUT MAINTAINING BOUNDARIES IN PROFESSIONAL SETTINGS?

BY COMMITTING TO PROFESSIONALISM AND KEEPING INTERACTIONS WORK-RELATED, YOU CAN REDUCE CONFLICTS AND MAINTAIN A MORE PRODUCTIVE AND RESPECTFUL WORK ENVIRONMENT.

Day	**13**

MANAGE YOUR EXPECTATIONS

DAY 13: ADJUST YOUR EXPECTATIONS ABOUT THEIR BEHAVIOR

OBJECTIVE	ACTIVITY	CONSIDER
RECOGNIZE THAT YOU CANNOT CONTROL OTHERS' ACTIONS, BUT YOU CAN CONTROL YOUR RESPONSES AND EXPECTATIONS, FOSTERING RESILIENCE AND MAINTAINING FOCUS ON PERSONAL GROWTH AND WELL-BEING.	REFLECT ON RECENT INTERACTIONS WHERE EXPECTATIONS WERE CHALLENGED. WRITE DOWN ONE EXPECTATION YOU HAD ABOUT SOMEONE'S BEHAVIOR THAT DIDN'T ALIGN WITH REALITY.	CONSIDER HOW ADJUSTING THIS EXPECTATION COULD LEAD TO MORE REALISTIC PERSPECTIVES AND LESS FRUSTRATION.

DEVELOP COPING STRATEGIES WHILE ADJUSTING EXPECTATIONS:
- ACTIVE LISTENING: STRIVE TO GENUINELY LISTEN TO THE OTHER PERSON'S PERSPECTIVE WITHOUT INTERRUPTING. REFLECT THEIR CONCERNS BACK TO THEM TO ENSURE UNDERSTANDING BEFORE OFFERING SOLUTIONS. FOR EXAMPLE, SUMMARIZING THEIR FEELINGS AND CONCERNS CAN DEMONSTRATE EMPATHY AND HELP BUILD RAPPORT.
- SEEK CLARIFICATION: IF THERE'S CONFUSION OR MISCOMMUNICATION, ASK CLARIFYING QUESTIONS TO ENSURE YOU UNDERSTAND THE SITUATION ACCURATELY BEFORE RESPONDING. THIS HELPS AVOID MISUNDERSTANDINGS AND PROMOTES EFFECTIVE COMMUNICATION.
- COMPROMISE ON TIMEFRAME: WORK TOWARDS ESTABLISHING A TIMEFRAME THAT ALL PARTIES CAN AGREE UPON. NEGOTIATE AND FIND A MIDDLE GROUND THAT CONSIDERS EVERYONE'S NEEDS AND CONSTRAINTS.
- FOCUS ON MAINTAINING YOUR OWN PROFESSIONALISM: STICK TO THE FACTS AND REMAIN COMPOSED.
- DOCUMENT: FOLLOW UP THE CONVERSATION WITH A WRITTEN EMAIL TO RECAP THE DISCUSSION AND ENSURE CLARITY.

Day	14

DEVELOP COPING STRATEGIES

DAY 14: IDENTIFY ONE NEW STRESS-RELIEF ACTIVITY

OBJECTIVE	ACTIVITY	CHOOSE
ENHANCE YOUR ABILITY TO HANDLE STRESS BY INCORPORATING NEW STRESS-RELIEF ACTIVITIES INTO YOUR ROUTINE.	IF 30 MINUTES OF CARDIO DOES NOT WORK FOR YOU (**DAY 8**), IDENTIFY A STRESS-RELIEF ACTIVITY THAT WORKS FOR YOU.	CHOOSE ONE NEW STRESS-RELIEF ACTIVITY TO TRY TODAY. EXAMPLES INCLUDE: • MEDITATION • JOURNALING • TAKING A NATURE WALK • LISTENING TO CALMING MUSIC • PRACTICING MINDFULNESS • DRAWING • PAINTING

SCHEDULE TIME:
SET ASIDE SPECIFIC TIME TODAY TO ENGAGE IN THE CHOSEN ACTIVITY.

REFLECT ON THE EXPERIENCE:
AFTER COMPLETING THE ACTIVITY, TAKE A FEW MOMENTS TO REFLECT ON HOW IT MADE YOU FEEL AND ITS EFFECTIVENESS IN RELIEVING STRESS.

- HOW DID THE NEW STRESS-RELIEF ACTIVITY MAKE YOU FEEL?
- DID IT HELP REDUCE YOUR STRESS LEVELS?
- WOULD YOU CONSIDER INCORPORATING THIS ACTIVITY INTO YOUR REGULAR ROUTINE?

BY TRYING NEW STRESS-RELIEF ACTIVITIES, YOU CAN DISCOVER EFFECTIVE WAYS TO MANAGE STRESS AND IMPROVE YOUR OVERALL WELL-BEING.

Day	15

BE PATIENT

DAY 15: REMIND YOURSELF THAT CHANGE IS GRADUAL AND REQUIRES PATIENCE

OBJECTIVE	ACTIVITY	PRACTICE
CULTIVATE PATIENCE BY UNDERSTANDING THAT CHANGE IS A GRADUAL PROCESS AND REQUIRES TIME.	REMIND YOURSELF OF THE GRADUAL NATURE OF CHANGE.	THROUGHOUT THE DAY, CONSCIOUSLY REMIND YOURSELF TO BE PATIENT IN YOUR INTERACTIONS AND EXPECTATIONS. USE POSITIVE AFFIRMATIONS, SUCH AS "CHANGE TAKES TIME" OR "I AM PATIENT AND PERSISTENT."

PROGRESS:
AT THE END OF THE DAY, REFLECT ON ANY PROGRESS MADE, NO MATTER HOW SMALL. APPRECIATE THE EFFORTS YOU AND OTHERS ARE MAKING TOWARD IMPROVEMENT.

REFLECT:
HOW DID REMINDING YOURSELF TO BE PATIENT IMPACT YOUR DAY?
DID YOU NOTICE ANY SMALL CHANGES OR PROGRESS IN YOURSELF OR YOUR INTERACTIONS?
HOW CAN MAINTAINING A PATIENT ATTITUDE BENEFIT YOUR LONG-TERM GOALS AND RELATIONSHIPS?

BY PRACTICING PATIENCE, YOU CAN BETTER MANAGE YOUR EXPECTATIONS AND CREATE A MORE POSITIVE AND RESILIENT MINDSET, ALLOWING FOR GRADUAL AND MEANINGFUL CHANGE.

Day	**16**

SEEK FEEDBACK

DAY 16: GAIN CONSTRUCTIVE FEEDBACK FROM A COLLEAGUE

OBJECTIVE	ACTIVITY	LISTEN AND REFLECT
CHOOSE A COLLEAGUE WHO YOU TRUST AND WHO IS FAMILIAR WITH YOUR INTERACTIONS AT WORK.	APPROACH THE TRUSTED COLLEAGUE AND EXPLAIN THAT YOU ARE SEEKING FEEDBACK TO IMPROVE YOUR INTERACTIONS WITH THE DIFFICULT CO-WORKER.	LISTEN CAREFULLY TO THE FEEDBACK WITHOUT INTERRUPTING OR DEFENDING YOURSELF. TAKE NOTES ON KEY POINTS AND REFLECT ON HOW YOU CAN USE THIS FEEDBACK TO IMPROVE.

REFLECT:
HOW DID RECEIVING FEEDBACK FROM YOUR COLLEAGUE MAKE YOU FEEL?
WHAT SPECIFIC POINTS OF FEEDBACK WERE MOST HELPFUL?
HOW CAN YOU APPLY THIS FEEDBACK TO IMPROVE YOUR FUTURE INTERACTIONS?

BY SEEKING FEEDBACK, YOU CAN GAIN VALUABLE INSIGHTS INTO YOUR BEHAVIOR AND COMMUNICATION, ALLOWING YOU TO MAKE MEANINGFUL IMPROVEMENTS AND BUILD STRONGER PROFESSIONAL RELATIONSHIPS.

AUTHOR'S NOTE: AVOID SHARING CONFIDENTIAL INFORMATION AND REFRAIN FROM GOSSIPING DURING THIS CONVERSATION. FOCUS ON THE FACTS AND ASK FOR FEEDBACK ON SPECIFIC INTERACTIONS. STAY OPEN TO THEIR INPUT, AS AN HONEST COLLEAGUE CAN OFFER VALUABLE PERSPECTIVES FROM ALL SIDES.

Day	17

BUILD YOUR RESILIENCE - POSITIVE SELF TALK

DAY 17: ENGAGE IN A RESILIENCE-BUILDING ACTIVITY

OBJECTIVE	ACTIVITY	SELF-TALK
STRENGTHEN YOUR ABILITY TO COPE WITH CHALLENGES BY ENGAGING IN RESILIENCE-BUILDING ACTIVITIES.	ENGAGE IN POSITIVE SELF-TALK. FOCUS ON AFFIRMING YOUR STRENGTHS AND ABILITIES.	SET ASIDE TIME TODAY TO PRACTICE POSITIVE SELF-TALK, WHETHER DURING A BREAK, COMMUTE, OR QUIET MOMENT.

EXAMPLES OF POSITIVE SELF-TALK INCLUDE:

- "I AM CAPABLE OF HANDLING DIFFICULT SITUATIONS."
- "I LEARN AND GROW FROM MY EXPERIENCES."
- "I STAY CALM AND COMPOSED UNDER PRESSURE."
- "I AM RESILIENT AND CAN OVERCOME OBSTACLES."
- "EVERY CHALLENGE I FACE MAKES ME STRONGER."
- "I FOCUS ON SOLUTIONS, NOT PROBLEMS."
- "I TRUST MYSELF TO MAKE THE RIGHT DECISIONS."
- "I AM IN CONTROL OF MY REACTIONS AND EMOTIONS."
- "I AM IN THIS ROLE FOR A REASON. I WORKED HARD FOR THIS."

BY PRACTICING RESILIENCE-BUILDING ACTIVITIES LIKE POSITIVE SELF-TALK, YOU CAN ENHANCE YOUR ABILITY TO NAVIGATE DIFFICULT SITUATIONS AND MAINTAIN A POSITIVE, PRODUCTIVE MINDSET.

Day 18

USE HUMOR

DAY 18: LIGHTEN THE MOOD WITH APPROPRIATE, CHEERFUL HUMOR

OBJECTIVE	ACTIVITY	APPROPRIATE
IMPROVE THE WORK ATMOSPHERE AND EASE TENSION BY USING APPROPRIATE, CHEERFUL HUMOR.	LOOK FOR MOMENTS DURING THE DAY WHEN A TOUCH OF HUMOR COULD LIGHTEN THE MOOD, SUCH AS DURING MEETINGS, CASUAL CONVERSATIONS, OR BREAKS.	ENSURE YOUR HUMOR IS RESPECTFUL AND SUITABLE FOR THE WORKPLACE. SHARE A LIGHT-HEARTED JOKE OR AMUSING ANECDOTE THAT EVERYONE CAN APPRECIATE.

OBSERVE THE IMPACT:
- NOTICE HOW YOUR USE OF HUMOR AFFECTS THE MOOD AND INTERACTIONS OF THOSE AROUND YOU

REFLECT:
- HOW DID USING HUMOR INFLUENCE THE ATMOSPHERE AND DYNAMICS AT WORK?
- DID IT HELP IN ALLEVIATING TENSION OR IMPROVING INTERACTIONS?
- WHAT TYPES OF HUMOR WORKED BEST IN YOUR WORKPLACE SETTING?

BY INCORPORATING CHEERFUL AND APPROPRIATE HUMOR INTO YOUR DAY, YOU CAN HELP CREATE A MORE POSITIVE AND ENJOYABLE WORK ENVIRONMENT.

AUTHOR NOTE: THIS IS MY FAVORITE, AS I ENJOY USING HUMOR TO LIGHTEN THE MOOD. HOWEVER, DURING 'WAYS OF WORKING' MEETINGS, I REFRAIN FROM USING HUMOR. THESE MEETINGS ARE TYPICALLY FOCUSED ON DISCUSSING LESSONS LEARNED AND MAKING DATA-DRIVEN DECISIONS.

Day	**19**

STAY GROUNDED

DAY 19: FOCUS ON THE BIG PICTURE AND LET MINOR IRRITATIONS GO

OBJECTIVE	ACTIVITY	PRACTICE
REMIND YOURSELF OF THE LARGER GOALS AND OBJECTIVES OF YOUR WORK.	REFLECT ON RECENT MINOR IRRITATIONS OR FRUSTRATIONS AT WORK.	CONSCIOUSLY DECIDE TO LET GO OF SMALL ANNOYANCES. USE TECHNIQUES LIKE DEEP BREATHING OR MINDFULNESS TO HELP YOU STAY GROUNDED.

AUTHOR'S NOTE: DURING A MEETING, WHENEVER THE SPEAKER SAID "UM," A CO-WORKER WOULD CLEAR THEIR THROAT, SEEMINGLY CORRECTING THE SPEAKER. I FOUND MYSELF HYPER-FIXATING ON THIS NEGATIVE ACTION. TO REGAIN FOCUS, I TOOK A COUPLE OF DEEP BREATHS AND REDIRECTED ALL MY ENERGY TOWARD LISTENING TO THE SPEAKER. I REMINDED MYSELF THAT MY GOAL WAS TO LEARN AND GAIN INSIGHTS FROM THE MEETING TO ACHIEVE MY OBJECTIVES. THIS SHIFT IN FOCUS HELPED ME REMAIN GROUNDED AND MAINTAIN PROFESSIONALISM, ALLOWING ME TO BENEFIT FROM THE MEETING DESPITE THE DISTRACTION.

IF YOU ENCOUNTER A SIMILAR SITUATION, PRACTICE DEEP BREATHING TO CENTER YOURSELF AND REFOCUS ON THE MEETING'S PURPOSE. REMIND YOURSELF OF YOUR GOALS AND THE VALUE OF THE DISCUSSION. REDIRECT YOUR ATTENTION AWAY FROM DISTRACTIONS AND TOWARD ACTIVELY PARTICIPATING AND LEARNING FROM THE CONVERSATION.

BY FOCUSING ON THE BIG PICTURE AND LETTING MINOR IRRITATIONS GO, YOU CAN MAINTAIN A CALMER, MORE BALANCED APPROACH TO YOUR WORK AND INTERACTIONS.

Day	**20**

BE ASSERTIVE

DAY 20: PRACTICE STANDING YOUR GROUND FIRMLY YET RESPECTFULLY

OBJECTIVE	ACTIVITY	UNDERSTAND
ENHANCE YOUR COMMUNICATION SKILLS BY PRACTICING ASSERTIVENESS, AND STANDING YOUR GROUND FIRMLY YET RESPECTFULLY.	THINK OF AN UPCOMING INTERACTION WHERE YOU CAN PRACTICE ASSERTIVENESS. THIS COULD BE A MEETING, A DISCUSSION WITH A CO-WORKER, OR A SITUATION WHERE YOU NEED TO EXPRESS YOUR NEEDS OR BOUNDARIES.	ASSERTIVENESS IS ABOUT EXPRESSING YOUR THOUGHTS, FEELINGS, AND NEEDS DIRECTLY AND RESPECTFULLY WITHOUT BEING PASSIVE OR AGGRESSIVE. IT INVOLVES STANDING UP FOR YOURSELF WHILE CONSIDERING THE NEEDS AND FEELINGS OF OTHERS.

PRACTICE ASSERTIVE COMMUNICATION:
- USE CLEAR, DIRECT LANGUAGE TO EXPRESS YOUR VIEWS.
- MAINTAIN A CALM AND RESPECTFUL TONE.

EXAMPLE PHRASES:
- "I FEEL MY CONTRIBUTIONS ARE BEING OVERLOOKED. I'D LIKE TO DISCUSS HOW WE CAN ENSURE EVERYONE'S INPUT IS VALUED."
- "I NEED MORE TIME TO COMPLETE THIS PROJECT EFFECTIVELY."

OBSERVE THE IMPACT:
- HOW DID OTHERS RESPOND TO YOUR ASSERTIVENESS?
- HOW DID IT AFFECT YOUR CONFIDENCE AND THE OUTCOME?
- WERE YOU ABLE TO STAND YOUR GROUND RESPECTFULLY?
- HOW CAN YOU IMPROVE FURTHER?

PRACTICING ASSERTIVENESS HELPS COMMUNICATE YOUR NEEDS AND BOUNDARIES, LEADING TO BETTER UNDERSTANDING AND RESPECT.

_____
_____
_____
_____
_____
_____
_____
_____

Day	21

AVOID POWER STRUGGLES

DAY 21: FOCUS ON THE ISSUE AT HAND RATHER THAN GETTING DRAWN INTO A CONFLICT OVER CONTROL

OBJECTIVE	ACTIVITY	UNDERSTAND
IMPROVE INTERACTIONS BY IDENTIFYING AND AVOIDING POWER STRUGGLES, FOCUSING INSTEAD ON CONSTRUCTIVE COMMUNICATION.	WHEN A CONFLICT ARISES, REMIND YOURSELF TO FOCUS ON THE PROBLEM, NOT THE PERSON.	POWER STRUGGLES OCCUR WHEN TWO OR MORE PEOPLE COMPETE FOR CONTROL, OFTEN LEADING TO UNPRODUCTIVE CONFLICT.

PLAN YOUR APPROACH:
DECIDE IN ADVANCE HOW TO AVOID ENGAGING IN THE POWER STRUGGLE. FOCUS ON COMMON GOALS AND SOLUTIONS RATHER THAN ON "WINNING" THE ARGUMENT.

IMPLEMENT STRATEGIES:
USE STRATEGIES SUCH AS ACTIVE LISTENING, STAYING CALM, AND SEEKING COMPROMISE.

REFRAME THE CONVERSATION:
SHIFT THE DIALOGUE TOWARD COLLABORATION AND MUTUAL GOALS. USE PHRASES LIKE, "HOW CAN WE SOLVE THIS TOGETHER?" OR "WHAT WOULD BE THE BEST OUTCOME FOR BOTH OF US?"

REFLECT:
WERE YOU ABLE TO FIND A MORE CONSTRUCTIVE AND COLLABORATIVE APPROACH?
WHAT DID YOU LEARN ABOUT HANDLING CONFLICTS AND MAINTAINING POSITIVE RELATIONSHIPS?

BY IDENTIFYING AND AVOIDING POWER STRUGGLES, YOU CAN FOSTER A MORE COOPERATIVE AND PRODUCTIVE WORK ENVIRONMENT.

	Day	22

FOCUS ON YOUR GOALS

DAY 22: FOCUS ON YOUR PROFESSIONAL GOALS AND ALIGN YOUR ACTIONS WITH THEM

OBJECTIVE	ACTIVITY	EXAMPLES
TO CLARIFY YOUR PROFESSIONAL GOALS AND ENSURE YOUR ACTIONS ARE ALIGNED WITH ACHIEVING THEM.	TAKE TIME TO REFLECT ON YOUR LONG-TERM AND SHORT-TERM PROFESSIONAL GOALS. DOCUMENT THEM CLEARLY AND SPECIFICALLY.	"EARN A PROMOTION TO TEAM LEADER WITHIN THE NEXT YEAR." "IMPROVE MY PROJECT MANAGEMENT SKILLS BY COMPLETING A CERTIFICATION COURSE." "EXPAND MY PROFESSIONAL NETWORK BY ATTENDING INDUSTRY EVENTS."

CREATE A PLAN:
DEVELOP A STEP-BY-STEP PLAN OUTLINING THE ACTIONS YOU NEED TO ACHIEVE EACH GOAL. SET DEADLINES AND MILESTONES TO TRACK YOUR PROGRESS.

REFLECT:
HOW DOES FOCUSING ON YOUR GOALS INFLUENCE YOUR DAILY ACTIONS AND DECISIONS?
ARE THERE ANY ACTIVITIES YOU NEED TO ADJUST OR ELIMINATE TO BETTER ALIGN WITH YOUR GOALS?
WHAT PROGRESS HAVE YOU MADE TOWARD YOUR GOALS, AND WHAT STEPS CAN YOU TAKE NEXT?

BY CLEARLY DEFINING YOUR PROFESSIONAL GOALS AND ALIGNING YOUR ACTIONS WITH THEM, YOU CAN MAINTAIN FOCUS AND DIRECTION IN YOUR CAREER, LEADING TO GREATER SUCCESS AND FULFILLMENT.

Day	23

BE PREPARED

DAY 23: PLAN FOR POTENTIAL CHALLENGES IN AN UPCOMING INTERACTION

OBJECTIVE	ACTIVITY	CONSIDER
ANTICIPATE AND PLAN FOR POTENTIAL CHALLENGES IN AN UPCOMING INTERACTION TO HANDLE THEM EFFECTIVELY.	CHOOSE AN UPCOMING MEETING, CONVERSATION, OR EVENT WHERE YOU ANTICIPATE POTENTIAL CHALLENGES.	CONSIDER PAST INTERACTIONS, THE PERSONALITIES INVOLVED, AND THE CONTEXT OF THE SITUATION • DISAGREEMENTS ON PROJECT DIRECTION • DIFFICULT QUESTIONS OR CRITICISMS • EMOTIONAL REACTIONS

PLAN YOUR RESPONSES:
DEVELOP STRATEGIES FOR ADDRESSING EACH ANTICIPATED CHALLENGE.

PREPARE CLEAR, CALM, AND ASSERTIVE RESPONSES TO POTENTIAL CRITICISMS OR CONFLICTS.
EXAMPLE STRATEGIES:
- STAY FOCUSED ON THE FACTS AND YOUR GOALS.
- HAVE DATA OR EXAMPLES READY TO SUPPORT YOUR POINTS.

PRACTICE:
IF POSSIBLE, REHEARSE YOUR RESPONSES WITH A TRUSTED COLLEAGUE OR MENTOR TO GAIN CONFIDENCE AND REFINE YOUR APPROACH.

REFLECT:
- HOW DID PREPARING FOR POTENTIAL CHALLENGES INFLUENCE YOUR CONFIDENCE AND READINESS?

BY ANTICIPATING AND PLANNING FOR POTENTIAL CHALLENGES, YOU CAN APPROACH INTERACTIONS WITH GREATER CONFIDENCE AND EFFECTIVENESS, LEADING TO MORE POSITIVE AND PRODUCTIVE OUTCOMES.

Day	**24**

LIMIT INTERACTIONS

DAY 24: MINIMIZE UNNECESSARY CONTACT WITH THE PROBLEMATIC CO-WORKER TODAY

OBJECTIVE	ACTIVITY	SET BOUNDARIES
MINIMIZE UNNECESSARY CONTACT WITH THE PROBLEMATIC INDIVIDUAL TO REDUCE STRESS AND IMPROVE PRODUCTIVITY.	REFLECT ON YOUR DAILY INTERACTIONS AND PINPOINT MOMENTS WHERE CONTACT WITH THE PROBLEMATIC INDIVIDUAL IS AVOIDABLE.	SET CLEAR BOUNDARIES TO MANAGE THESE INTERACTIONS EFFECTIVELY. COMMUNICATE THROUGH EMAIL INSTEAD OF HOLDING FACE-TO-FACE MEETINGS. ARRANGE MEETINGS ONLY WHEN ABSOLUTELY NECESSARY, AND PRIORITIZE GROUP SETTINGS OVER ONE-ON-ONE DISCUSSIONS.

COMMUNICATE PROFESSIONALLY:
WHEN INTERACTIONS WITH A DIFFICULT CO-WORKER ARE NECESSARY, KEEP THE CONVERSATION FOCUSED STRICTLY ON WORK-RELATED TOPICS.

REFLECT ON THE PROCESS:
HOW DID LIMITING YOUR INTERACTIONS AFFECT YOUR STRESS LEVELS AND PRODUCTIVITY? WERE YOU ABLE TO MAINTAIN PROFESSIONALISM DURING THESE ESSENTIAL CONVERSATIONS?

AUTHOR'S NOTE: SETTING BOUNDARIES WITH A CHALLENGING CO-WORKER WAS A TOUGH BUT NECESSARY STEP FOR ME. WHENEVER THEY ADDED MEETINGS TO MY CALENDAR, I MADE IT A POINT TO INVITE OTHER TEAM MEMBERS. THIS APPROACH NOT ONLY HELPED ME MANAGE THESE INTERACTIONS MORE EFFECTIVELY BUT ALSO FOSTERED A SUPPORTIVE TEAM DYNAMIC. IT SIGNIFICANTLY REDUCED MY STRESS AND ALLOWED ME TO STAY FOCUSED ON MY PRIORITIES, GIVING ME THE MOTIVATION AND HOPE TO KEEP MOVING FORWARD.

| Day | 25 |

STAY INFORMED

DAY 25: REVIEW YOUR WORKPLACE POLICIES ON BEHAVIOR AND CONFLICT RESOLUTION

OBJECTIVE	ACTIVITY	APPLY
ENHANCE YOUR UNDERSTANDING OF WORKPLACE POLICIES ON BEHAVIOR AND CONFLICT RESOLUTION.	REVIEW WORKPLACE POLICIES: ASK YOUR HUMAN RESOURCES OR A TRUSTED SOURCE TO SHARE THE WRITTEN POLICIES WITH YOU.	CONSIDER HOW YOU CAN APPLY THIS INFORMATION TO HANDLE CURRENT OR FUTURE CHALLENGES EFFECTIVELY. IDENTIFY WAYS TO PROMOTE A RESPECTFUL AND POSITIVE WORK ENVIRONMENT BASED ON POLICY GUIDELINES.

REVIEW WORKPLACE POLICIES:
- PAY ATTENTION TO GUIDELINES ON RESPECTFUL CONDUCT, REPORTING PROCEDURES FOR CONFLICTS, AND AVAILABLE RESOURCES.

UNDERSTAND PROCEDURES:
- FAMILIARIZE YOURSELF WITH THE STEPS INVOLVED IN ADDRESSING CONFLICTS OR INAPPROPRIATE BEHAVIOR.
- NOTE WHO TO CONTACT FOR ASSISTANCE OR MEDIATION IF NEEDED.

REFLECT:
- WHAT DID YOU LEARN FROM REVIEWING THE WORKPLACE POLICIES?
- HOW CAN YOU UTILIZE THIS KNOWLEDGE TO IMPROVE YOUR INTERACTIONS AT WORK?
- ARE THERE ANY CHANGES OR ACTIONS YOU NEED TO TAKE BASED ON THIS REVIEW?

BY STAYING INFORMED ABOUT WORKPLACE POLICIES, YOU CAN NAVIGATE CONFLICTS MORE CONFIDENTLY AND CONTRIBUTE TO A HARMONIOUS WORKPLACE CULTURE.

Day	26

ENCOURAGE COLLABORATION

DAY 26: SUGGEST A TEAM PROJECT OR COLLECTIVE GOAL TO FOSTER TEAMWORK

OBJECTIVE	ACTIVITY	PROPOSE
FOSTER TEAMWORK AND IMPROVE RELATIONSHIPS BY SUGGESTING A TEAM PROJECT OR COLLECTIVE GOAL.	THINK OF A PROJECT OR GOAL THAT ALIGNS WITH YOUR TEAM'S OBJECTIVES AND INTERESTS. ENSURE IT REQUIRES INPUT AND EFFORT FROM MULTIPLE TEAM MEMBERS.	PRESENT THE PROJECT IDEA TO YOUR TEAM EITHER DURING A MEETING OR VIA GROUP EMAIL. HIGHLIGHT THE ADVANTAGES OF COLLABORATION AND EXPLAIN HOW WORKING TOGETHER CAN EFFECTIVELY ACHIEVE SHARED GOALS.

DEFINE ROLES AND RESPONSIBILITIES:
CLEARLY OUTLINE EACH TEAM MEMBER'S ROLE AND RESPONSIBILITIES. ENSURE EVERYONE UNDERSTANDS HOW THEIR CONTRIBUTION IS CRUCIAL TO THE PROJECT'S SUCCESS.

SET MILESTONES AND DEADLINES:
ESTABLISH CLEAR MILESTONES AND DEADLINES TO KEEP THE PROJECT ON TRACK. SCHEDULE REGULAR CHECK-INS TO DISCUSS PROGRESS AND ADDRESS ANY CHALLENGES.

REFLECT:
HOW DID YOUR TEAM RESPOND TO THE IDEA OF A COLLABORATIVE PROJECT?
DID THIS APPROACH HELP IMPROVE TEAMWORK AND RELATIONSHIPS?
WHAT POSITIVE OUTCOMES DID YOU OBSERVE FROM FOSTERING COLLABORATION?

ENCOURAGING COLLABORATION THROUGH TEAM PROJECTS OR COLLECTIVE GOALS CAN STRENGTHEN RELATIONSHIPS, ENHANCE COMMUNICATION, AND CREATE A MORE SUPPORTIVE AND PRODUCTIVE WORK ENVIRONMENT.

| Day | 27 |

RESOLUTION SKILLS

DAY 27: LEARN ONE NEW CONFLICT RESOLUTION TECHNIQUE

OBJECTIVE	ACTIVITY	LEARN
ENHANCE YOUR ABILITY TO HANDLE DISPUTES EFFECTIVELY BY LEARNING A NEW CONFLICT RESOLUTION TECHNIQUE.	RESEARCH VARIOUS CONFLICT RESOLUTION TECHNIQUES SUCH AS ACTIVE LISTENING OR MEDIATION.	STUDY THE STEPS INVOLVED IN YOUR CHOSEN TECHNIQUE. UNDERSTAND THE PRINCIPLES AND STRATEGIES BEHIND IT.

LEARNING THE "WIN-WIN" APPROACH:

I REMEMBER A TIME WHEN OUR TEAM WAS DIVIDED OVER HOW TO ALLOCATE RESOURCES FOR AN IMPORTANT PROJECT. TENSIONS WERE HIGH, AND IT SEEMED LIKE NO ONE WAS WILLING TO COMPROMISE. I DECIDED TO LEARN ABOUT THE "WIN-WIN" APPROACH, A CONFLICT RESOLUTION TECHNIQUE POPULARIZED BY STEPHEN COVEY IN HIS BOOK THE 7 HABITS OF HIGHLY EFFECTIVE PEOPLE. THIS APPROACH FOCUSES ON FINDING SOLUTIONS THAT SATISFY ALL PARTIES INVOLVED.

I BEGAN BY ACTIVELY LISTENING TO MY CO-WORKER'S CONCERNS AND NEEDS. INSTEAD OF FOCUSING ON WHAT I WANTED, I AIMED TO UNDERSTAND THEIR PERSPECTIVES DEEPLY. THEN, I FACILITATED A BRAINSTORMING SESSION WHERE WE GENERATED SOLUTIONS THAT COULD ADDRESS EVERYONE'S INTERESTS. BY ENCOURAGING OPEN COMMUNICATION AND CREATIVE THINKING, WE FOUND A WAY TO DISTRIBUTE RESOURCES THAT EVERYONE COULD AGREE ON.

USING THE "WIN-WIN" APPROACH NOT ONLY RESOLVED THE CONFLICT BUT ALSO STRENGTHENED OUR TEAM'S COLLABORATION AND TRUST. IT WAS A VALUABLE LESSON IN THE POWER OF SEEKING MUTUALLY BENEFICIAL SOLUTIONS.

Day	28

PRACTICE GRATITUDE

DAY 28: WRITE DOWN THREE THINGS YOU ARE GRATEFUL FOR TODAY

OBJECTIVE	ACTIVITY	EXAMPLES
ENHANCE YOUR EMOTIONAL WELL-BEING BY FOCUSING ON POSITIVE ASPECTS OF YOUR LIFE.	REFLECT ON YOUR DAY AND IDENTIFY THREE THINGS YOU ARE GRATEFUL FOR - THESE CAN BE SMALL OR LARGE, PERSONAL OR PROFESSIONAL.	I AM GRATEFUL FOR A SUPPORTIVE COLLEAGUE WHO HELPED ME WITH A PROJECT. I AM GRATEFUL FOR A PEACEFUL LUNCH BREAK THAT ALLOWED ME TO RECHARGE. I AM GRATEFUL FOR THE OPPORTUNITY TO LEARN SOMETHING NEW TODAY.

DURING A PARTICULARLY STRESSFUL TIME AT WORK, I DECIDED TO START A DAILY GRATITUDE JOURNAL AS I STRUGGLED TO FIND THINGS TO BE THANKFUL FOR AMIDST THE CHAOS. ONE EVENING, AFTER A LONG AND CHALLENGING DAY, I SAT DOWN WITH MY LAPTOP, FEELING OVERWHELMED. I TOOK A DEEP BREATH AND DECIDED TO FOCUS ON THE SMALL, POSITIVE MOMENTS I OVERLOOKED THAT DAY.

I HAD A BRIEF BUT UPLIFTING CONVERSATION WITH A COLLEAGUE WHO COMPLIMENTED MY RECENT WORK. I TYPED OUT MY FEELINGS, REALIZING HOW MUCH THAT SMALL RECOGNITION MEANT TO ME.

I ALSO NOTED THE BEAUTIFUL SUNRISE I WITNESSED ON MY WAY TO WORK, WHICH MOMENTARILY FILLED ME WITH A SENSE OF PEACE.

LASTLY, I EXPRESSED GRATITUDE FOR THE COMFORTING CUP OF COFFEE I ENJOYED DURING MY DRIVE TO WORK, WHICH PROVIDED A MUCH-NEEDED MOMENT OF RELAXATION.

AS I CONTINUED THIS PRACTICE, I FOUND THAT EVEN ON THE MOST CHALLENGING DAYS, THERE WERE ALWAYS MOMENTS OF GRATITUDE. THIS SIMPLE HABIT HELPED SHIFT MY PERSPECTIVE, ALLOWING ME TO FOCUS ON THE POSITIVE ASPECTS OF MY LIFE RATHER THAN GETTING BOGGED DOWN BY THE NEGATIVES.

Day 29

BE FLEXIBLE

DAY 29: ADAPT YOUR APPROACH BASED ON WHAT WORKS BEST IN A GIVEN SITUATION

OBJECTIVE	ACTIVITY	IDENTIFY
ENHANCE YOUR ABILITY TO HANDLE DIVERSE SITUATIONS BY ADAPTING YOUR APPROACH.	THINK OF A RECENT CHALLENGING SITUATION AT WORK. CONSIDER HOW YOU INITIALLY APPROACHED IT AND THE OUTCOME.	IDENTIFY ALTERNATIVE APPROACHES BY BRAINSTORMING DIFFERENT WAYS THE SITUATION COULD HAVE BEEN HANDLED AND CONSIDERING HOW FLEXIBILITY MIGHT HAVE IMPROVED THE OUTCOME.

CHOOSE AN UPCOMING SITUATION WHERE YOU CAN PRACTICE BEING FLEXIBLE BY ADAPTING YOUR APPROACH TO WHAT YOU BELIEVE WILL WORK BEST IN THAT SPECIFIC CONTEXT. WHEN FACED WITH CONFLICTING IDEAS OR PREFERENCES, PRACTICE NEGOTIATING TO FIND MUTUALLY AGREEABLE SOLUTIONS. THIS FLEXIBILITY IN FINDING COMPROMISES NOT ONLY STRENGTHENS RELATIONSHIPS BUT ALSO ENHANCES TEAMWORK.

AS YOU MOVE THROUGH DIFFERENT SITUATIONS, REGULARLY EVALUATE YOUR APPROACH AND THE OUTCOMES. USE ANY FEEDBACK OR INSIGHTS GAINED TO ADJUST YOUR STRATEGIES, REFINING YOUR RESPONSES FOR FUTURE INTERACTIONS.

BY EMBRACING FLEXIBILITY, YOU CAN MORE EFFECTIVELY NAVIGATE THE UNPREDICTABLE NATURE OF INTERACTIONS WITH A DIFFICULT CO-WORKER, MAKING IT EASIER TO HANDLE CHALLENGES WITH GREATER SUCCESS.

_____
_____
_____
_____
_____
_____
_____
_____

Day	30

KNOW WHEN TO WALK AWAY

DAY 30: REFLECT ON YOUR LIMITS AND CONSIDER IF WALKING AWAY MIGHT BE NECESSARY

OBJECTIVE	ACTIVITY	EVALUATE
RECOGNIZE AND RESPECT YOUR PERSONAL BOUNDARIES BY UNDERSTANDING WHEN IT MIGHT BE NECESSARY TO WALK AWAY FROM A SITUATION.	CONSIDER PAST INTERACTIONS AT WORK AND IDENTIFY SITUATIONS WHERE YOU FELT YOUR LIMITS WERE BEING PUSHED.	THINK ABOUT A CURRENT OR UPCOMING INTERACTION WITH A DIFFICULT PERSON. ASSESS IF THE SITUATION IS DETRIMENTAL TO YOUR WELL-BEING OR IF IT HAS REACHED A POINT WHERE NO PRODUCTIVE OUTCOME IS LIKELY.

PLAN YOUR NEXT MOVE:
- ENSURE YOUR NEXT MOVE IS SOLIDIFIED, SUCH AS HAVING A CONTRACT SIGNED OR A CLEAR COURSE OF ACTION IN PLACE.
- CONFIRM THAT THE STEPS ARE WELL THOUGHT OUT AND READY BEFORE PROCEEDING.

CONSIDER WALKING AWAY:
- PLAN HOW TO EXIT THE SITUATION GRACEFULLY AND PROFESSIONALLY IF NECESSARY.

REFLECTION:
- WHAT ARE THE POTENTIAL BENEFITS AND CONSEQUENCES OF WALKING AWAY?
- ARE THERE OTHER STRATEGIES YOU COULD TRY BEFORE DECIDING TO WALK AWAY?

SAFETY NOTE:
- ENSURE YOUR PLAN INCLUDES CONSIDERATIONS FOR YOUR SAFETY AND WELL-BEING.

AUTHOR'S NOTE: KNOWING WHEN TO WALK AWAY IS A CRUCIAL SKILL FOR MAINTAINING YOUR MENTAL AND EMOTIONAL HEALTH. IT EMPOWERS YOU TO PROTECT YOUR WELL-BEING AND PRIORITIZE YOUR PEACE OF MIND WHEN FACED WITH CHALLENGES. TAKING THIS STEP CAN LEAD TO A HEALTHIER, MORE FULFILLING WORK ENVIRONMENT.

Conclusion

Following this 30-day checklist helps you effectively manage a difficult co-worker while gradually developing your necessary skills and resilience. This process empowers you to positively influence your work environment, all while prioritizing your mental health and professional goals.

Having navigated this challenging path, I understand the daily toll of dealing with confrontational people. There were moments when I felt defeated, doubting my ability to cope. However, I rediscovered my strength and confidence through consistent effort, reflection, and the strategies outlined in this checklist.

You're not alone in this struggle. Each day you commit to this checklist is a significant step toward a healthier work life and a stronger version of yourself. Approach this journey with an open heart and determination. Every small victory is a testament to your resilience and bravery.

Stay committed, trust your ability to overcome challenges, and know you're laying the foundation for lasting personal and professional growth.

Thank you for choosing this guide. I'm grateful for the opportunity to be a part of your journey toward a more empowered and fulfilling work life.

About the Author | MP

Meredith Poczkalski is a career coach, author, and podcast host dedicated to helping individuals navigate life's challenges with humor, resilience, and practical insights. With a wealth of experience in the retail industry, Meredith brings relatable stories and actionable advice to professionals and everyday listeners alike.

Meredith co-hosts two unique and widely popular podcasts with her friend and collaborator, Cassandra:

"The Clopen Effect: A Funny Retail Podcast", where Meredith and Cassandra share hilarious and heartfelt stories from the retail world, offering a behind-the-scenes look at the quirks, challenges, and joys of the industry.

"Anxiety Makes Me Poop," a space where the duo invites listeners to laugh and heal together, diving into conversations about anxiety, self-care, and finding balance in a chaotic world.

Through their podcasts, Meredith and Cassandra create a safe, engaging, and entertaining environment where listeners feel seen, supported, and inspired to tackle challenges with confidence and humor.

When she isn't writing, coaching, or podcasting, Meredith enjoys spending time with her family, exploring new places through travel, and going for a long run.

Whether connecting with her audience or sharing a good laugh, Meredith believes resilience and humor are key ingredients for personal growth and professional success.

Your Notes

"Coming together is a beginning. Keeping together is progress. Working together is success." — Henry Ford

"None of us is as smart as all of us." — Ken Blanchard

"Collaboration allows us to know more than we are capable of knowing by ourselves." — Paul Solarz

"If you want to go fast, go alone. If you want to go far, go together." — African Proverb

"Teamwork divides the task and multiplies the success."
— Unknown

"A team is not a group of people who work together. A team is a group of people who trust each other." – Simon Sinek

"Surround yourself with a trusted and loyal team. It makes all the difference." — Alison Pincus

"A group becomes a team when each member is sure enough of themselves and their contribution to praise the skills of others."
— Norman Shidle

"The best teamwork comes from men who are working independently toward one goal in unison." — James Cash Penney

www.ingramcontent.com/pod-product-compliance
Lightning Source LLC
Chambersburg PA
CBHW070207230526
45471CB00002B/866